DK ESSENTIAL MANAGERS

Selling

ERIC BARON

London, New York, Melbourne, Munich, and Delhi

Senior Editor Peter Jones
Senior Art Editor Helen Spencer
Executive Managing Editor Adèle Hayward
Managing Art Editor Kat Mead
Art Director Peter Luff
Publisher Stephanie Jackson
Production Editor Ben Marcus
Production Controller Hema Gohil
US Editor Margaret Parrish

Produced for Dorling Kindersley Limited by

cobaltid

The Stables, Wood Farm, Deopham Road,
Attleborough, Norfolk NR17 1AJ
www.cobaltid.co.uk

Editors Louise Abbott, Kati Dye, Maddy King,
Marek Walisiewicz
Designers Darren Bland, Claire Dale, Paul Reid,
Annika Skoog, Lloyd Tilbury, Shane Whiting

First American Edition, 2009

Published in the United States by DK Publishing
375 Hudson Street, New York, New York 10014

09 10 11   10 9 8 7 6 5 4 3 2 1

ND130—February 2009

Published in Great Britain by
Dorling Kindersley Limited.

A catalog record for this book is available from
the Library of Congress.

ISBN 978-0-7566-4196-2

DK books are available at special discounts
when purchased in bulk for sales promotions,
premiums, fund-raising, or educational use.
For details, contact: DK Publishing Special Markets,
375 Hudson Street, New York, New York 10014 or
SpecialSales@dk.com.

Color reproduction
by Colourscan, Singapore
Printed in China by WKT

Discover more at **www.dk.com**

Contents

CHAPTER 2

Understanding the needs of customers

CHAPTER 3

Making your recommendations

CHAPTER 4

Resolving objections and closing the sale

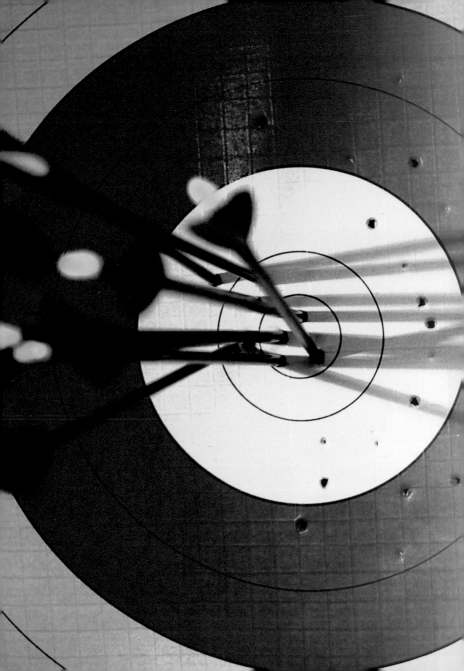

Introduction

Selling is a time-honored profession and one that constantly moves with, and adapts to, broader changes in business practice, human interactions, and psychology. Selling is also—as every salesperson will tell you—the cutting edge of every business. Without the eyes, ears, and intuition of a good salesperson, the business itself founders.

Every good salesperson knows their products inside and out—whether these are paper clips, aircraft engines, or consultancy services—and can present them capably to their customers. However, a great salesperson does so much more. He or she understands the customers' needs and brings a problem-solving mentality and real creativity to all interactions.

Selling is all about combining a set of attitudes, behaviors, and skills in a way that forges long-term relationships with customers—relationships that add value to the customer's business and that yield not just one deal, but many.

Despite some bad press over the years, selling is a worthy profession. The goal of this book is to open your mind in a way that helps you approach selling in a very different way and that introduces you to skills you must demonstrate every day. Let the journey begin!

Chapter 1

Building meaningful relationships

People buy from people whom they like, respect, and trust, so selling is really about building and managing relationships. The first step is to find out what your customers expect and demand, and what you need to do to respond accordingly.

Adding value through selling

Offering good products at competitive prices just isn't enough to win sales in today's competitive market. Your can bet that your best ideas will be emulated by others sooner or later. Today's customers expect you to add value to their business—to address their needs and deliver solutions.

The evolving selling mentality

Being a successful salesperson today involves you in collaboration, facilitation, and a sense of partnership with your customer. Long gone are the days of one-way persuasion—the canned pitch is considered the lowest level of selling. Ideas about selling have evolved rapidly as globalization and fast communication have produced more savvy and demanding buyers. Selling reflects wider changes in business and today goes far beyond pushing product, embracing an understanding of how organizations work, management structures, psychology, and self-awareness.

TIP

Understanding your role

THINK CREATIVELY
Don't limit yourself to thinking about only your products and services—your customers need your creativity to help solve their problems.

In the past, a salesperson could get by through eloquently telling the customer everything he or she knew about their product, and explaining why their company was the best in its field. This approach may still win you business today in some areas, but most customers now demand much more from their salespeople. They expect them to add value to their business—to understand fully their needs and to offer up solutions to problems they didn't even realize they had. To succeed, you need to interpret what the client tells you, and often educate your customer about what's out there. Then you need to mesh together the abilities of your organization with that of the client for the benefit of both. You need a measure of curiosity and good listening skills to uncover what the client really needs. And you must be a brilliant innovator, with the ability to think creatively and manage creative processes that find answers.

IN FOCUS... SELLING PROFILE

There's no formula for a great salesperson—they come from all walks of life and levels of society. However, salespeople share some characteristics that make them more likely to succeed:
• **Willingness to take risks**—putting their own necks on the line and entering unchartered waters to come up with unique ideas.
• **Generosity**—giving credit to others where deserved without reservation, and sharing credit without fear of diminishing individual contribution.
• **A thick skin**—knowing how to deal with failure and understanding that even the best lose more often than

they win. With experience, salespeople learn how to deal with inevitable negative responses to their ideas, as well as their own innate emotional responses to knockbacks.
• **A methodical approach**—understanding that planning and follow-up are the keys to success.
• **Resourcefulness**—constantly innovating and challenging the existing approaches. Salespeople work well in groups and make the most of the talent around them.
• **Tenacity**—knowing that daunting problems cannot be tackled without effort and determination.

Addressing needs

Selling isn't a moment of inspiration; it is not about force of argument or the strength of your personality. It is a process. The process is fairly easy to understand, but—as you'll see—hard to do. The techniques in this book are centered around a process called needs-based selling, so let's examine its principles and set the scene.

REFRAME THE SALES VISIT

Think of every sales call as a problem-solving opportunity. You are selling more than products and services; you're selling ideas, perspectives, and insights.

Examining the process

The process of selling requires careful planning and management. Beginning a relationship with a new client is the first phase of the process: you can't just walk into a customer's office and kick off a sales meeting—it needs careful staging, and both you and your customer need to be prepared.

Next, you start the most important part of the sales process—determining the customer's needs. During this phase, you ask the key questions, listen to what the customer has to say, identify both the obvious and less obvious needs, enter into a meaningful dialogue, and review what you have learned. Needs determination drives everything in selling, and it is only once you have listened to your customer that you move on to the phase of the process that most salespeople enjoy the most: presenting their products and services. This is when you get to explain how you and your company can address your customer's needs. You know your products and services inside-out, and your customers want to hear how you can help them.

Once you have determined the needs and made recommendations, it is time to think about gaining commitment. But something almost always gets in the way—and you face resistance to commit. The customer needs to be allowed to object—even when they seem ready to buy—and you must resolve the client's objections if you are to close the sale.

Needs-based selling

Simply put, needs-based selling means determining a customer's needs before you start to propose solutions. Get to understand the customer by letting them speak—at length, if necessary. When it's time to present, you'll do a better job than those who merely display their products and services and you'll be far better positioned to sustain a long-term customer relationship.

Solving problems

Success in selling is linked to effective problem solving. If you're good at one, the chances are that you'll excel at the other. The process of problem solving is also remarkably similar in its structure to that of selling (see below), further reinforcing the link.

COMPARING PROBLEM SOLVING WITH SELLING

STEP	PROBLEM SOLVING	NEEDS-BASED SELLING
1	Set the stage. Provide structure for the problem-solving session.	Open the meeting. Build rapport, confirm the agenda, prepare the customer.
2	Define the problem. Review background information and solutions already tried.	Determine needs. Engage with the client and tease out both their obvious and their hidden needs.
3	Generate ideas. Provide the climate where everyone can contribute creative perspectives without judgment.	Present products and services. Describe the features and benefits of what you have to sell. Impart your enthusiasm and belief in your products.
4	Evaluate the ideas and develop the best ones. Identify the appealing aspects of an idea, then list the concerns.	Resolve objections. Effectively and sensitively resolve the objections that customers inevitably raise.
5	Summarize the solution. Put together a specific action plan.	Close the deal. Agree on how to move forward with fulfillment.

Appealing to buyers

Countless studies have addressed the central questions of sales—why do buyers buy? How do customers make decisions? What do they demand from salespeople? The answers come down to three discernable behaviors: believing in your position, empathy, and trust.

TIP

SET THE TONE
You don't have to be funny to be successful in sales, but it helps to be fun. Be the kind of person who brightens up a room when they enter, as opposed to the person who brightens up a room when they leave it.

Establishing your position

People buy from people who know their stuff. If the salesperson can't consistently demonstrate that he or she knows what they are talking about, it becomes almost impossible to buy from them.

Put yourself in the buying role. You want to buy a new refrigerator, but the salesperson just can't explain why model A is better for you than model B. Chances are that you'll shut down as a customer; in fact, you'll probably want to leave and go to a different store. Knowing what you sell inside-out is a given, but your credibility extends far beyond product knowledge. You must become familiar with your customer's business, competitors, industry, and marketplace. You need to be well prepared. It's not hard—almost everything you need to know about your customers and markets is readily available online.

✔ CHECKLIST GAINING RESPECT BY SHOWING RESPECT

	YES	NO
• Do you show respect for your client's space by, for example, avoiding placing objects on their desk?	☐	☐
• Do you show respect for their business by, for example, asking before you take notes?	☐	☐
• Do you show respect for your competitors? If you put down one of the client's existing suppliers, you are disrespecting the client.	☐	☐

Showing empathy

Empathy is the ability to connect with someone—to see things from their perspective. Several recent studies indicate that, for many buyers, a salesperson's ability to understand their situation is the single most compelling reason why they make the decision to buy.

Many people think that empathy depends on similarity of age, background, experience, or point of view. That's a myth. A young salesperson can connect with and relate to someone much more senior if they can identify areas of mutual interest. It's not hard to find common ground. For starters, both are already in the same business—even if they are on different sides of the desk. They may have similar interests and educations: if salespeople allow the customer to talk and genuinely show interest in what they say, the customer will appreciate the empathy shown.

Without understanding the customer and showing real interest in what he or she has to say, a key ingredient in the relationship will be missing and the salesperson will remain an order taker... at best.

GET IN TOUCH
Focus on empathy. Management guru David Maister famously said: "Customers don't care how much you know until they know how much you care."

Building trust

Trust takes a long time to build, but only a second to lose. To demonstrate that you can be trusted, you need to be responsive, direct, clear, reliable, and straightforward. Customers don't like to be manipulated and don't appreciate evasiveness. If you get caught being dishonest in any way, you'll not only lose that customer, but the ripple effect of your actions will also spread far beyond the borders of that relationship.

Always assume that your customer is smart and give them due respect: don't play games, make sure to deliver on your promises, and avoid nasty surprises. Follow these simple rules and your customer's trust will follow in time.

Ways to mitigate risk and build trust

START SMALL
Don't ask for all the business; ask for a piece of it. Show the customer your capabilities and earn the business over time.

IDENTIFY PARALLEL SITUATIONS
Review a similar situation with the customer and demonstrate how it worked previously.

Managing risk

You know that you are trustworthy, and your customer thinks you are trustworthy. Good start. Being considered trustworthy and actually being trusted to fulfill a million-dollar contract are two different things. US consulting firm Synectics® Inc. carried out some inspired research that accounts for the difference between these two concepts—it is summarized in the trust formula:

$$trust = \frac{credibility \times intimacy}{risk}$$

The formula shows that your ability to demonstrate credibility and build relationships is directly proportional to trust. But trust is inversely proportional to the level of risk involved in making a decision—how much the client has to lose. The top of the equation is within your control. To be successful in sales, you need to demonstrate credibility (see above) and intimacy, which is comprised of behaviors such as empathy, affability, sensitivity, and likeability. Intimacy speaks to how safe and secure it is to work with you.

So it's the lower part of the equation—risk—that's less within your control and works against your ability to build relationships. To be successful, you must effectively learn to manage risk.

With that in mind, you as a salesperson must constantly ask yourself what you can do to make any commitments less risky for the customer. Remember the old adage: "Nobody ever got fired for hiring IBM." That's because the risk was much lower in hiring Big Blue than a less-established high-tech company.

BUILD IN AN EXIT STRATEGY
Let the customer know there will be a way to get out of the situation if things don't work out as planned.

EXPLAIN THE WORST CASE
Make the client aware of all the risks and how you'll do your best to keep them under control.

REASSURE THE CUSTOMER
Tell them you'll be there throughout the process; if anything goes awry you'll be ready to take action if necessary.

TAKE THE BURDEN
Stand behind what you are doing for the customer; let them know you will take full responsibility if things go wrong.

SHARE THE RISK
Enlighten the customer about the risk for you—if things don't happen as anticipated, you'll pay a price as well. Convey that "we're in it together."

GUARANTEE RESULTS
Or at the very least, guarantee your commitment to stick together throughout the process.

Differentiating yourself

Whether you're selling computer support, pharmaceuticals, or plumbing supplies, chances are that your competitors offer similar products at equal or better prices with identical backup. You need to do everything to set your product apart from the others, and there is no better way to differentiate your company than through your approach to your customer.

Providing more than the goods

To be a success in sales, you should constantly ask yourself what you can do to add value to the client relationship. If all you do is facilitate the supply of products and services, you are not adding value— just reacting. Even when you provide solutions to known problems, you are still in reactive mode and are not adding much value. This begins only when you help the customer to determine their needs.

The goal is to move up the value chain to become a strategic adviser to your customer—someone the customer calls for guidance, ideas, perspective, insights, and, quite simply, help. Once you rise to that level with a customer, your position is rock solid.

BE FIRST
Do whatever you can to keep yourself on the customer's mind, by emailing or sending personal notes and letters. Your customers don't think about you as much as you think about them, so ensure they think of you first when the opportunity arises. But beware—don't become annoying.

Achieving visibility

Make yourself visible to your customer. To rise to the level of a trusted adviser and differentiate yourself from your competition, visit your customers in person on a regular basis. This approach has many benefits: it strengthens the relationship with your customer; it gives you an opportunity to learn their needs directly and through nonverbal clues; and it enables you to see firsthand who your customer regularly interacts with in their organization and the many facets of their work life that remain hidden on the phone.

Surprising your customers

Aim to give your customers something they did not ask for or expect. Let them know that you care a bit more than anyone else, that you are willing to do things others haven't even thought about, and that you are not just concerned about getting the sale. Tom Peters, the world-renowned customer-service guru, talks about "wowing and delighting customers." Showing them you are different can be what ultimately tips the scales in your favor when you and your competitor are running neck and neck.

? ASK YOURSELF... AM I "WOWING" MY CUSTOMER?

- Are there any relevant articles or pieces of research that you could send them?
- Can you put them in touch with a third party who can provide something you can't?
- Do you know of any suppliers who could help them reduce their costs?
- Can you help them solve a pressing problem?
- Is there a significant personal event that you could acknowledge?
- Do you know someone who is looking to change careers who they might like to meet?

Chapter 2

Understanding the needs of customers

Almost every sales professional worth his or her salt acknowledges the key importance of understanding their customers' needs. But what does this really mean, and how do you achieve it in the real world?

Implementing the model

The concept of needs-driven or needs-based selling is nothing new. Corporations have always boasted about their ability to develop products that address their customers' needs, and the concept has been incorporated into sales training programs for decades. Why then, is needs-based selling often so poorly implemented?

PRACTICE YOUR SKILLS

When you are in non-business situations with friends or family, ask yourself what their needs are relative to your discussion. It helps you become better at identifying needs and can make you a better friend.

Breaking the 80/20 rule

"Do you understand all of your customers' needs?" In surveys, more that 80 percent of salespeople answer "yes" to this question. Yet studies of their customers reveal that, seen from the client's side, only 20 percent of salespeople are addressing needs. Some people call this startling discrepancy in perceptions the "80/20 rule." As a salesperson, you need to understand why this happens, and what you can do to make sure that you're part of the successful 20 percent.

Taking your time

So why is it that so many salespeople respond in a way that their clients don't want? The answer is—in part—that they are too eager. Early in a sales meeting, they hear a need from a customer and, with the best of intentions, start to address it, start to provide a solution. You ask: "Isn't that what needs-driven selling is all about?" Not exactly: if you hear a need and respond to it immediately, it's a little like reading the first chapter of a book and drawing conclusions regarding the author's message. You know a bit—but just that; the whole story awaits. Any premature recommendation is likely to miss the mark, resulting in a disappointed customer.

It takes a lot of self-confidence to step back and admit to yourself and your client that you're not yet prepared to make a recommendations. You need to acknowledge that you don't understand your customer as well as you thought and that you need to ask more questions. This level of humility doesn't come naturally to most salespeople.

ASK YOURSELF...
HOW DO I TUNE IN TO A CLIENT'S NEEDS?

Each time you interact with a customer, ask yourself these types of questions to put yourself in the right mindset:

• What is this person trying to accomplish?
• What does he or she really want from me?
• What are their primary concerns?
• What's holding them back?
• What are they getting/not getting from their current supplier(s)?
• What gaps exist in their current relationship(s)?
• Why are they taking the time to see me?

Seeing the nature of needs

Before you start questioning your customer to uncover his or her needs, it helps to know what these needs might look like—and how they are likely to present themselves. You'd be surprised at how even the most seasoned sales professionals have difficulty recognizing needs.

ANALYZE YOUR THOUGHT PROCESS

Whenever you find yourself offering a solution to a customer, ask yourself what the need is that led to this solution. You'll be amazed at how taking one step back will leave you two steps forward.

Separating needs from solutions

The respected Harvard economist Theodore Levitt famously said: "Nobody needs a drill, they need a hole." In other words, people's real needs are sometimes hidden behind apparent solutions. A simple example may help illuminate what Levitt was getting at. Imagine you own a travel agency. A customer walks in days before the winter vacation; he's in a panic because he hasn't arranged that big vacation he promised his wife and children. You listen patiently. He says the family is so excited but he's worried that he's left the arrangements too late. He tells you that the vacation is hard to plan because his three children have such different interests—from going to museums to rock climbing—while his wife just needs to have some down time. He brags about how the cost issue is not a big deal to him.

CASE STUDY

New blood for Citibank
In the early 1980s, Citibank was one of the first major financial organizations to attempt the creation of a unique sales culture. The Consumer Banking Group interviewed many of the largest sales training companies, but—to the surprise of many—hired a young, small, and virtually unknown firm to lead the charge. When the decision-maker was asked why she chose that firm, her response was simple: "Of all the firms we interviewed, they did the best job of demonstrating that they understood our needs. And if that's what we want to teach our people, let's go with people who practice what they preach." Enough said.

TIP

SELL BLANKS

Approach some sales calls as if you were "selling without a product." This forces you to focus strictly on the customer—a productive habit to get into.

When salespeople hear stories like this, many immediately start thinking up solutions. "What can we offer him that will address all his issues? If he wants to spend more, let's help him—it's more commission for us. 'What your family needs, sir, is a spa vacation in Dubai.'"

This might indeed be a satisfactory solution, but the salesperson has done little to understand the customer's needs. A little analysis, and further questioning might reveal that the client has a need to impress and be respected by his family; to act quickly; to carve out some adult time on his vacation; to have a safe, supervised environment; and many other needs besides. Taking this longer approach has real benefits: the customer feels understood and valued; he'll buy this vacation from you, and come back for your guidance and advice, year after year.

"My family can't agree on what sort of vacation we should have."

"Katie and Maddy love sports but Shane is much happier exploring, and Louise just wants to relax."

"I know I've left it late, but it has to be something that keeps both my kids and my wife happy."

"No problem. Let's start by exploring what you need a little further. What were the best things about your last vacation?"

BE SENSITIVE
After each meeting, ask yourself what the customer didn't say. You'll probably unearth some needs they did not consciously know they had.

Reading between the lines

Sometimes your customers will tell you exactly what they need. All you have to do is listen and respond. But if you address only these overt needs, you are not adding much value to the client, and you are doing no more than any of your competitors would do. Where you can differentiate yourself—and win the client's respect and trust—is by hearing and responding to implied needs. So your task is to look for the needs behind what the customer says. For example, if the client complains about his boss constantly second-guessing him, he may be expressing a need to have a solid, tightly reasoned explanation for his buying decisions. Successful sales professionals know how to uncover these implicit needs—indeed, it is what drives their long-term success.

Selling would be a far easier task if customers could be relied on always to buy for sound business reasons—such as return on investment, quality, value, and competence. If the buyer always made his or her decision dispassionately, rather than based on how that decision made them feel, reading their requirements would be straightforward.

BUSINESS AND PERSONAL NEEDS

Business needs are measurable while personal needs are subjective. Below are some examples of each to illustrate the differences between the two.

BUSINESS NEEDS	PERSONAL NEEDS
Reduce cost	Look good in front of peers
Increase efficiency	Gain recognition
Shorten production time	Get that promotion
Become more effective	Minimize the risk
Increase profitability	Boost personal status
Improve turnaround time	Decrease stress

However, all customers—however company-focused they may be—are to some extent influenced by personal needs. These delve into areas that are harder to quantify—security, connecting with others, ego, and comfort. For this reason, showing empathy with the customer will bring you rich rewards.

Beginning the questioning

Before you begin to question your client to determine their needs, let them know why you need the information, how it will benefit them, and how it relates to the agenda. Explain that by answering your questions they will:
• Help you focus on the right issues.
• Allow you to make better recommendations.
• Get an the opportunity to outline their concerns.
• Ensure that you learn about them.
They are more likely to be open and honest with their answers if they understand the structure of the needs determination process (see right).

Asking, and asking again

Many pieces of research on the selling process point to one simple conclusion: the more questions you ask of your client, the more success you'll enjoy—the person who learns the most needs is primed to win the business. But the corollary is that the longer you manage a relationship, the more likely you are to lose sales. That is because, over time, you become complacent, making assumptions about the customer rather than asking questions. That's why many salespeople report a falling share of sales, just when they thought the relationship was thriving. The bottom line is to keep asking questions consistently, methodically, and creatively.

HOW TO... FIND OUT CLIENT NEEDS

Introduce the questioning session

Ask the right questions

Listen for the needs

Review and check the needs

TIP

RECOGNIZE MOTIVES

Look out for customers who are risk averse, or who appear to worry about how they are going to appear; they tend to be driven more by personal needs.

Planning your approach

Most sales managers agree that the margins separating good, very good, and excellent salespeople are not dependent upon what happens face-to-face, but what happens before and after the sales process. You may feel energized and ready to jump right into a sales meeting with a new customer, but if you spend time planning the content and thinking through the process, your chances of success will be greatly enhanced.

Doing your homework

The first stage of planning is getting your content right—ensuring that you have all the information you need for every stage of the sales process.

Start your preparation by determining the objectives of the meeting, both for you and the customer. Once these are established, ask yourself what you already know about the customer and what you still need to learn. There is no excuse for not knowing what is going on in your customer's industry and marketplace. There are many sources of data that you can tap to make sure you are prepared, including—but not limited to—annual reports, product brochures, articles, press clippings, industry magazines, and trade show summaries. Check out your customer's website

Questions to prepare you for the sales meeting

Who?
- Who makes the decisions?
- Who should I see?
- Who will do what from our side?

What?
- What questions will I ask?
- What drives this customer's decisions?
- What ideas will I suggest?
- What objections do I anticipate?

and try to get a sense of what changes are on the horizon in their business. Find out about their competitors, key in on what the marketplace is saying, and understand what your customers are demanding.

If appropriate, think about what you want to recommend to the customer, and the corresponding features and benefits. Try to anticipate objections and ask yourself what the real issues might be and what answers you may be able to provide.

Preparing the process

Getting the content right is important, but you also need to plan how to manage the selling process—the way you deliver the information. Consider all the stages of the selling process, from opening the meeting to closing the deal. Do you know what you will do and say in each one and how you will manage the transitions between the phases? Feeling relaxed and well prepared is crucial, so rehearse your presentation repeatedly, and ask for feedback from colleagues. Practice delivering your questions, resolving objections, and even closing. This will highlight any areas in which you are less than confident, and reveal any holes in the information you need to succeed.

Where and when?

- Where is the best place to conduct the meeting?
- When would be the most effective time?

Why?

- Why is this approach good for our business?
- Why are we targeting this specific customer?

How?

- How will I run the meeting?
- How can I differentiate us from our competitors?

Making your first move

It has lots of names—the initial contact, the cold call, the first call, the canvas, the exploratory call, and others. That first visit to a prospective customer can be a daunting, even scary, experience for most people early in their careers. The good news is that this does change over time.

HOW TO...
MAKE INITIAL IMPACT

Get the lead

↓

Write your letter of introduction

↓

Make the call and secure an appointment

↓

Confirm the appointment in writing

↓

Make the initial visit

↓

Send a follow-up letter

Finding the way in

You can't set up a first meeting until you have a lead. Experiment with finding different sources of leads:
• Former customers
• Referrals from existing customers
• Newspaper articles and industry publications
• Trade shows/symposiums
• The "dead file"—prospects others have given up on
• Centers of influence (third parties).
    Armed with leads, your key prospecting tool will be the letter. You can justify three of these in the prospecting process; one to introduce yourself, one to confirm an appointment to meet, and one to follow up on the initial meeting. Emails are fine once you have a relationship, but send a traditional letter for the initial approach—it will set you apart from the competition.

Making an appointment

In some industries, it can be acceptable just to drop by, but regardless of the business you are in, you will be more successful if you obtain an appointment first. Send a confirmation letter, letting the customer know you are looking forward to meeting them and confirm the date, time, and time allocation. Review your own agenda and include some relevant material for the customer to look at. Encourage them to invite anyone who might benefit from attending.

Creating an impression

Your first meeting with a new prospect may have many purposes—from a simple introduction to a full-blown sales call. Whatever happens, stay calm and begin the process of understanding your potential customer's needs. You should try not to present anything specific (although you should be prepared to present your company's credentials; see next page). Instead, establish rapport, and let the customer do most of the talking.

HAVE FUN

Try thinking of cold calls as fun: you'll never know exactly what to expect, so be ready for anything and take pride in your ability to respond to the situation. It's a new beginning… so be sure to make it a memorable one.

Learn what you can about the individual and their business. Look for, and reinforce, common ground. Are they familiar with your company? Is there any relevant history between your organizations that could form a bond? Do you share interests or acquaintances in the industry?

MAKING THE FIRST VISIT

FAST TRACK

OFF TRACK

FAST TRACK	OFF TRACK
Being humble—you haven't been there before	Showing unfounded familiarity—it's only the first meeting
Showing appreciation for the customer taking the meeting	Acting like you are entitled to be there
Doing your homework and demonstrating what you have learned in preparation for the visit	Treating this meeting as if it were just another meeting
Confirming the meeting in writing to show interest	Just showing up without putting in the preparation time
Asking lots of questions of the customer and letting them talk	Presenting specific recommendations

Presenting your credentials

Despite your best intentions to focus on the customer's needs, you will often find that you are asked to give a quick explanation of who you are and what you have to offer—a credentials presentation—before the customer will give you any information about themselves.

Aiming for needs first

A credentials presentation is an overview of your company, what it does, and how it adds value to its customers. You need to be prepared to give a brief presentation, but if you can avoid having to do so at this early stage of your relationship with a customer, you should: as soon as you start talking about how to help them before identifying and confirming their needs, it becomes more about you than about them. If your customer says to you: "Tell me about your company," it can sometimes work to respond with: "I'll be delighted to explain who we are and how we may be of assistance, but I can do that much more effectively if I learn a bit about you first." If the customer agrees, you can start the needs-determination process; if not, you will have to make a credentials presentation.

TIP

KEEP IT GENERAL

Use the presentation to give a brief overview of needs you can fulfil and of your product line, but don't make any assumptions about the specifics needs of your customer.

"Our products address a range of needs"

Getting the message right

A good way to build a credentials presentation is to use your team—not just the sales team, but anyone in the business who would like to contribute. Ask different members of the team to put themselves in the position of a customer of your company, and talk to you about what they would like to hear. As you build your presentation, practice it with the team: discuss how it sounds and tweak it until you get it right.

The key to a successful credentials presentation is to keep it short and to the point. Don't overload the customer with information—you will (hopefully) have the opportunity to provide detail later. Give some history about the company and yourself. If you have an interesting anecdote about how the company started, don't be afraid to share it. In a general sense, aim to tell them the kinds of things you do and the kinds of companies you work with, and briefly outline your success stories. Discuss needs in general, and then explain why what you have to offer can be of value to a company like theirs. Words such as "can," "could," or "might" are the most appropriate because you have not yet learned enough about your customer to get specific.

✔ CHECKLIST **PREPARING A CREDENTIALS PRESENTATION**

	YES	NO
• Have you discussed with your team how you want to position your company to people who aren't familiar with what you do?	☐	☐
• Have you used your company's mission and vision statements to provide key facts and figures?	☐	☐
• Have you trimmed your presentation so that it can be delivered within a few minutes?	☐	☐
• Have you practiced in front of a friend or colleague until you are fully confident in your delivery?	☐	☐

Opening a sales meeting

When you make an appointment to see a client—whether it is your first or your fiftieth—you are effectively calling a meeting for that customer. For the meeting to run well, you need to take the initiative, while at the same time acknowledging that the meeting belongs to the customer—it must be focused on providing solutions to their problems.

Building rapport

What happens in the first few minutes of a sales visit sets the tone for the entire meeting. It helps to break the opening down into three critical steps: building rapport, confirming the agenda, and moving into the meeting itself.

At the start of the meeting, make sure everyone is comfortable, knows who is who, and has a chance to connect informally. Encourage small talk or a discussion of general business conditions. Use your intuition to decide when to move on—you need to work at your customer's comfort level, not your own. Here are a few ideas to help you get off to a good start:

• Look around the client's office for something to trigger conversation, such as a picture or trophy.

• Compliment the customer on their office or facility—but you must be sincere.

• Thank the customer for their time.

• Discuss something you know about their business—a relevant news event, for example—to show that you've done your homework.

IN FOCUS...
TALKING TO THE RIGHT PERSON

Surprisingly, two-thirds of all sales calls are made to people who do not make or implement decisions. Salespeople are often reluctant to ask a prospect whether they are speaking to the person who is responsible for calling the shots, for fear of sounding disrespectful. The following preamble can help you check if you're talking to the right person: "I visit many organizations like yours and everyone has their own way of making decisions. To ensure that I don't waste anyone's time or leave someone out of the loop, would you please share with me how the process works here?"

Setting the agenda

Next, ensure that everyone is clear about the objectives of the meeting. Even though this is a sales call, it requires a clear agenda, distributed in advance, that takes into account your needs and your client's (remember, it is their meeting). Give each person the opportunity to express their interest in the meeting and what they would like to get out of it. This is crucial: you may not realize the status or position of a participant in your meeting, and run the risk of missing out on a huge opportunity.

Finally, confirm the time available for the meeting, and stick to it. Customers resent people who overstay their welcome.

Guiding the meeting

Old-style salespeople were loath to lose control of a meeting and so did all the talking and tried to force the customer on to their agenda. You can see now that this isn't consistent with a problem-solving approach to selling. Instead, you should acknowledge that the meeting belongs to the customer—you are there to solve their problems, after all. Your role is more as facilitator, to ensure that the meeting runs smoothly. Once you begin addressing issues on the agenda, ensure that the meeting stays focused on the stated purposes. Try to draw out ideas from all participants, then move the meeting toward an action plan and schedule the follow-up.

Roles in the sales meeting

THE SALESPERSON
- **Facilitates the meeting**
- **May take minutes**
- **Participates in finding solutions**

THE CLIENT
- **Owns the problem**
- **May chair the meeting**
- **Participates in finding solutions**

Questioning for needs

Of all the skills demanded of a successful salesperson, questioning remains the most important. This is simply because you can't hope to understand a customer's needs without asking questions in a thoughtful, credible, and sensitive way.

Running the session

When you question a customer at a sales meeting, you need to keep the session light—think of it as an open discussion rather than an interrogation. Comfortable customers invariably reveal more— and more useful—information.

The questions you ask to determine needs fall into three broad categories—fact-finding questions, needs-oriented questions, and big-picture questions— each of which are considered below. There are no hard-and-fast rules about the types of question to ask

---

CASE STUDY

Asking the right questions

One of the classic stories in the sales business recalls how Pepsi Cola won the airline business from Coca Cola in the 1990s. At the time, Coca Cola owned the in-flight business and there was no way Pepsi could win the business in a price war. The new national sales manager was about to make his first visit to one of the airlines and had prepared a lavish and thoughtful presentation. At the last minute, one of his internal resources suggested that they show up with only a pad and pen—no presentation at all.

Against his better judgment, he agreed. For two hours, all they did was ask questions and learn about the airline. They hardly mentioned Pepsi. They learned that beyond ensuring safety, the biggest need the airline had was to sell more tickets. They had uncovered a critical need that had to be met if they were to be successful in their bid for the business.

They developed a plan to give retailers coupons that allowed them to buy airline tickets at a discount: at the time, this was a unique approach that departed from the pattern of typical promotions. The airlines loved the idea, awarded Pepsi the business, and in the first year alone were able to sell more than $2 million in additional tickets. A legendary result.

your customer, but experience suggests that a ratio of around five fact-finding questions, to three needs-oriented questions, and one big-picture question is comfortable for the client and achievable for you.

Finding the facts

To scope out an account or manage a relationship, you need some fundamental pieces of information about the client—their customers, partners, suppliers; their company structure; number of employees; and so on. These questions may seem obvious, but it's surprising how often they are overlooked. These are usually closed questions that can be answered "yes" or "no" or with a fact. Their job is to elicit information, so they tend not to be all that imaginative (virtually everybody asks them), but can be surprisingly provocative (for example, "Who makes the decisions here?"). They are essential, but they won't do a whole lot to differentiate you from your competition.

Probing the needs

Needs-oriented questions get the customer talking and are far more open ended. They can be quite imaginative—"If you could change one thing about the way you do business today, what would that be?"—or even provocative. Typically, these questions do not have "right" or "wrong" answers; they open up new areas of discussion, and will absolutely help differentiate you from your competition.

Responses from the customer will encompass everything from their objectives, goals, hopes, expectations, and aspirations to their problems, concerns, worries, and fears. As your relationship with the client evolves, you can ask progressively deeper questions that will help reinforce trust.

TIP

LEARN FROM THE PROS

Watch the great interviewers on television. They ask short questions and don't give the person being interviewed possible answers. They ask a question and stop talking; try the same technique.

Learning about the big picture

Big-picture questions position you to uncover needs that the customer does not necessarily know he or she has. They are strategic in nature, in essence asking the customer to think about things that they may not like to consider—the future of the business, difficulties to be overcome, the need to plan, contingencies, and long-term goals. Big-picture questions require planning on your part because they can lead to uncomfortable—albeit valuable—discussions. They are necessarily thought-provoking, and will stay in the customer's mind for a long time. They elevate the conversation and will eventually result in your being perceived as an adviser or consultant—much more than a salesperson.

TIP

BEWARE OF THE "WHY?"
Be careful of questions that begin with a "why"—they can appear judgmental and put people on the defensive: it helps to introduce them with a preamble.

Planning the ask

Most people are naturally suspicious of questions. When determining needs, you should be as sensitive as possible during the process of questioning your client.

• Give a preamble: let the customer know that questions are coming, why you are asking, and how it is in their interests to answer.

• Cluster questions into categories, focusing on strategy, finance, inventory, and so on, each with its own preamble.

• Be straightforward in your questions.

• Don't shy away from the tough questions.

Questions to investigate the client's needs

FACT-FINDING
- What are your annual sales?
- Who are your current suppliers?
- How often do you purchase?
- How much do you with this account?
- Who makes the decisions?

NEEDS-ORIENTED
- What are your expectations of someone like me?
- What changes are you initiating to stay competitive?
- How has globalization impacted your business?
- What are some of the biggest challenges you face today?
- How has your customer base changed?

BIG-PICTURE
- What is your vision for the company?
- Where would you like the company to be in five years?
- What obstacles could prevent that from happening?
- How do you see yourself leveraging your strengths in the long-term?
- How will you ensure that you benefit from globalization?

Listening to your client

You can ask your client brilliantly incisive questions to determine their needs. But these are worth little if you don't listen to their responses. Listening isn't easy—studies reveal that we retain a tiny percentage of what we hear—but it is a critical skill for any salesperson.

TIP

ASK FIRST
Always ask if it's OK to take notes and show respect for confidentiality. Clients will rarely decline and will probably be flattered that you want to record what they say.

Keeping tuned in

As a salesperson, you are the eyes and ears of your organization; what you learn about your client in a sales meeting will make your company stand or fall. You should be listening at a high level all the time—collecting facts, information, and business-related concepts—but most of all, listening for needs. Of course, this is the ideal scenario, and in reality your ability to listen is jeopardized by many factors. Instead of listening, you may start anticipating the next question, planning your response, or trying to understand what the customer meant. You may get distracted thinking about your route home or tomorrow's meetings; and there are biological reasons why attentive listening is harder than it seems—we think much faster than we can talk. But whatever your reason for tuning out, you can be sure that when you do, you're missing vital information.

CASE STUDY

Showing interest
Four out of five clients think that when you don't make notes, you aren't fully engaged. This research is borne out by a story related by a sales manager, who, along with a colleague, began a sales meeting with a prospective client. Neither was taking notes. After a few awkward minutes, the client called his assistant on the phone and said: "Please bring two pads and two pens for our guests since I would like to have the impression that they are at least somewhat interested in what I have to say." This is a true story—don't let this happen to you!

Making notes

There are many ways to enhance your listening skills, of which one of the best known is Active Listening*— a concept that has been around more than half a century and is explored in dozens of courses and books. A simple and, arguably, more effective technique can be set out in just two words—Take Notes, or more accurately, Make Notes. From the minute the customer starts talking, you should put pen to paper. The distinction between "taking" and "making" notes is important because you are doing more than just recording the client's words—you are jotting down any connections you make, and capturing on paper the need, the concern, the issue, the opportunity. Don't analyze too much—there will be plenty of time for reflection later.

The discipline of making notes has further benefits—it stops you from trying to respond too early, and it ensures that you listen to the customer throughout the meeting—it's a fact that many people "save the best for last," revealing their deepest needs toward the end of a conversation. If you present too early, chances are you'll miss hearing vital information.

*Active Listening— *a structured form of listening that focuses attention on the speaker. A listener consciously attends fully to the speaker and then repeats in their own words what he or she thinks the speaker has said, often interpreting the speaker's words in terms of feelings.*

Approaching a problem

Bringing a problem-solving approach into your dealings with customers has clear benefits. But how do you put it into practice? Problem solving seems intangible and difficult, but following a structured process, such as the technique of brainstorming, will bring focus to your interactions with customers and increase your chances of sales success.

TIP

MAKE SPACE FOR INNOVATION

Don't overdefine a problem. Usually, if people learn too much about a problem, they will become less willing to speculate and will find themselves putting on the same blinkers that the problem owner already has.

Setting the scene

Problem solving requires creativity—but that doesn't mean chaos. When you bring together a group to develop creative solutions, you need to give the meeting structure. Be sure to define the task, decide what approach you use and how much time is available, and establish who is chairing, facilitating, and keeping minutes of the meeting.

Next, the group should identify the problem and set it into a proper context of background information. Why is the problem a problem? Could it be turned into an opportunity? Has the problem been addressed before, and how? Who is responsible for results? Once the meeting has been staged and the problem defined, the group is ideally positioned to generate ideas through brainstorming.

IN FOCUS... BRAINSTORMING

When it is done right, the technique of brainstorming taps people's capacity for lateral thinking and free association and boosts creative output. The concept was conceived in the 1920s by Alex Osborn, partner in international advertising agency BBDO (he was the "O" in the company). Osborn summarized the technique in the statement: "It is easier to tone down a wild idea than to think up a new one." Many precede their brainstorming sessions with creativity or relaxation exercises to help participants move into a more creative state.

Encouraging creative solutions

When you begin a brainstorming session, invite ideas, perspectives, recommendations, and insights. Encourage participants to be speculative and open—the meeting should be energetic, exciting, and fun. Resist any temptation to evaluate ideas as soon as they are put forward—anything goes. The opportunity to be innovative invariably yields richer results than if individuals feel constrained by rules and limitations.

Evaluating results

Brainstorming is a great way to spend the first half of a problem-solving session. The second part must be devoted to selecting the most exciting ideas and evaluating them diligently to develop solutions.

The evaluation process doesn't have to be complex, but it does have to be managed with care. Once an idea has been selected, the challenge becomes how to turn it into a solution.

One of the most common approaches suggests first identifying the appealing aspects of an idea and then listing concerns. Identifying the positives ensures that you have captured and preserved the parts of the idea that you want to save. Then address each concern, beginning with the most troubling, until the idea becomes acceptable. At this point, when the idea has been transformed into a solution, carefully summarize your conclusions and put together a specific action plan that includes the next steps to implement the results.

Reviewing needs

The perfect way to complete the Needs Assessment and move into the presentation phase is to demonstrate to the customer that you have been listening, that you understand what they have been saying, and that you're in tune with what they hope to accomplish.

TIP

SEEK CONFIRMATION

If there are several people in the room, check with each of them that your understanding of the needs matches theirs. Just because one person agrees with you it doesn't mean they all do.

Selling before presenting

Everything you have done up to this point has been focused on learning the needs of your customer. But before you start to present your solutions, you should demonstrate a clear understanding of his or her situation. If you review the needs well, you'll demonstate credibility, empathy, sensitivity, and trustworthiness—and many buyers will make their decision to buy at this point, even before you have presented your goods and services. Conversely, without thoroughly reviewing the needs, you risk misunderstanding your client and missing the mark with your recommendations.

CHOOSING YOUR WORDS

⬆ FAST TRACK	⦸ OFF TRACK
"Here's my understanding of what you said…"	"What you need is…"
"I may be reading too much into this, but it appears that…"	"You said that…"
"How I interpreted X's statement was that you had a desire to…"	"X told us that you wanted…"

Q IN FOCUS... THE PSYCHOLOGY OF LISTENING

Carl Rogers (1902–1987) was one of the world's greatest psychologists and students of human communication. He famously said that the "greatest compliment one human being can pay another is to demonstrate that he was listening." When a sales professional takes the time to review with a customer his or her understanding of their needs, they are indeed paying a great compliment and differentiating themselves—yet again—from the competition, in an emphatic manner.

Ensuring a close match

When you begin the review, choose your words carefully: tell the client what you heard as opposed to what they said. The distinction is subtle, but avoids putting words in the client's mouth (see box, opposite). Start by summarizing the client's overt needs and move to those you need to infer. Ask the client to confirm that your review is correct, and request that they prioritize their needs. Ask if you missed anything, if there's anything they'd like to add, or if your understanding is flawed. You just might pick up another need along the way.

Timing the review

The best time to review needs is either at the end of a needs-determination meeting or at the beginning of a meeting in which you are presenting (especially if new people are present, or a lot of time has passed since the last meeting). Concluding a meeting by reviewing needs ends it on a positive note and sets the stage for the next meeting when you will present. If you have done everything right, the client will already have a strong inclination to buy from you.

Selling with others

Bringing a colleague with you—whether it's your manager, a subject expert, another member of the team, or the new salesperson who just joined the company—can potentially make your sales meeting much more effective. However, joint sales meetings need to be managed carefully if they are to live up to their potential.

Being prepared

Preparation is the key to effective joint sales meetings. First, anyone you bring with you to the meeting needs to have a full understanding of its objective. At the very least, they need to know who the customer is, what they do, where you are in the relationship, and what you hope to accomplish. Equally importantly, your colleagues need to be clear about what their role in the meeting will be, or you run the risk that they will be unprepared. Are they there to ask questions, make recommendations, help deal with objections, or just to show support and interest?

Managing a joint meeting

In a joint sales meeting, it is even more important that you act as the facilitator, managing the process and trying to ensure that both your objectives and your customer's are fulfilled. Get the meeting off to a positive start by inviting introductions: make sure that everyone knows who everyone else is and that all are clear about what each party hopes to accomplish. During the meeting, it is important that every member of your team makes a contribution, so call on your colleagues when their expertise is needed, and explain why: "I would like John to answer that question since it falls within his area of expertise."

Benefits of joint sales meetings

SPECIALIZED KNOWLEDGE
Inviting colleagues from different functional areas of your organization to join you at the meeting allows you to offer a greater range of expertise to the customer.

LOOKING GOOD
Bringing a team—especially if it includes senior members of your organization—may impress the customer, and make them feel that they are important to you.

TWO PAIRS OF EARS
Sales meetings can be fast paced, especially if you are acting as the facilitator. If you have a colleague with you, they can pick up on small details that you may miss.

DIFFERENT PERSPECTIVES
With more than one of you interpreting what the customer is saying, you may get a fuller understanding of the customer's needs.

IMPROVING PERFORMANCE
Your colleagues can give you feedback on your performance, enabling you to be even more effective at your next sales meeting.

Chapter 3

Making your recommendations

Providing solutions and making recommendations is the part of the selling process that most salespeople like best. It's time to demonstrate how you can help the customer, to tell your story, and to present your products and services.

Using features and benefits

Client presentations take many forms; they range from informal one-to-one meetings to formal expositions to a conference room full of potential clients. Surprisingly, regardless of the situation, your approach will not vary that much: your presentation will focus on features and benefits.

Defining the terms

Salespeople have used features and benefits to describe their products and services for many decades. This approach has stood the test of time for one reason—it works!

Features tell customers how products or services work. They are characteristics, descriptions, attributes, specifications, and explanations. Benefits explain how the product helps—why it is important to the client and how it addresses their needs. Benefits set out to the customer the value of the item being discussed and why it is in their interests to purchase it.

Selling the benefits

People make the decision to buy things because of their benefits rather than their features. However, most salespeople are more comfortable talking about features than benefits. It's not hard to see why. Features are facts and hard to debate. You will rarely be challenged when you explain the features of a product or service—they are tangible and objectively notable.

Benefits, on the other hand, are educated guesses. They are subjective—what might be a benefit for one person may not be a benefit for another. Talking benefits makes some people uncomfortable, because it feels like a "hard sell". It shouldn't. Benefits do no more than explain why a recommendation makes sense.

When you make your presentation, think in terms of benefit statements and always try to link your features to the benefits. If you don't, you're only telling half the story. The example below—where a salesperson presents a new design of a stacking chair—shows the types of connections to make.

Linking features and benefits

FEATURE OF CHAIR	BENEFIT OF CHAIR
Neat, stackable design	Saves space, making it ideal for even the smallest venues
Metal legs	Durable—has a lifespan twice as long as close competitors, saving money
Stiffened back	Enhanced comfort and better sitting position—ideal for longer conferences
Discreet handle	Easy to carry and reposition—gives more flexibility at the venue.

Targeting the pitch

Features and benefits are the trusted selling tools that address the client's questions "What?" and "So what?" But if you can answer one further question—"What's in it for me?"—you'll set yourself apart from the competition. This question addresses the specific benefit—the particular needs of an individual customer.

TIP

HOLD BACK THE BROCHURES

Try using your sales brochure after you have presented, not before. Highlight the areas where your products meet the client's needs.

Focusing on specifics

Your ability to express the features and benfits of your products is vital, but there's one more conceptual step to take—understanding and presenting specific benefits. Every customer buys for slightly different reasons: some base their decisions on quality, convenience, and price; others on the level of service, or personal reasons that reflect how they feel about themselves. Specific benefits speak to the confirmed, most important, needs of a particular client; they differ from generic benefits, which make broader statements about the value of a product or service.

Prioritizing your messages

Information about your products and services and their corresponding features and benefits is fixed information—it's what you might include in your brochure, spec sheet, or catalog. By contrast, the needs of each customer and the specific benefits you present are variable. This variable information is at the heart of the needs-driven selling process—it's what elevates your presentation far above the canned pitch.

So, when the time comes to present, deliver the variable information first. Start by succinctly reviewing the customer's needs; next, make recommendations and demonstrate how they address the customer's needs—the specific benefits. Only when this is done should you move on to presenting the generic features and benefits. At first glance, this ordering of the information appears backward—going from the specific to the general. However, it addresses the reality of your audience's attention span. High-level listening efficiency lasts a frighteningly short time—up to 90 seconds—before dipping precipitously. Specific benefits are what close deals, so be sure to get them in early, before your client's attention wanders.

HOW TO... ORDER YOUR PITCH

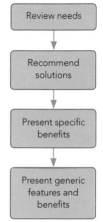

IN FOCUS... THE HUMAN TOUCH

Back in the 1960s, social forecasters were predicting that salespeople would be made obsolete by the turn of the century through advances in computing and revolutionary marketing vehicles, such as direct mail and telemarketing. They could not have been more wrong. More people are selling today than ever before, and even professions that never considered using the "s" word in the past, such as banking, accounting, law, and medicine, find themselves soliciting business on a day-to-day basis. That's because the consumer does not want to buy from a catalog, a piece of mail, or a voice on the telephone. They want to buy from a person who listens to them, understands their needs, and responds with appropriate products and services.

Offering your ideas

Many sales professionals think that all they have to offer is their products and services. But it's not just what's in your bag that's important—it's what's in your head. When you present your customer with an idea that helps them do their job a bit better, teaches them something new, or addresses a personal issue, you are building value in your relationship that lets you leapfrog way ahead of your competitors.

Giving to receive

When a sales professional presents a customer with an idea that has no revenue attached to it, it's called an uncompensated idea. This is a great misnomer, because surprising your customers with novel and unexpected thinking accumulates great value and brings long-term financial reward. If you're prepared to give, you will receive.

ASK YOURSELF... **ABOUT OFFERING NEW IDEAS**

Before each client meeting, think of areas in which you could help the client by offering uncompensated ideas.

- Are they doing something that we know they could do better with better technology or software?
- What problems do they consistently raise—how hard is it for me to research them?
- Is there something in the client's nonworking life where I could offer an idea—for example, suggesting a venue for their child's party?
- Is there something about the client's facility that could be improved—a lack of signage, for example?
- Can I enhance the client's industry knowledge—by recommending a good seminar or training program?

Salespeople are often reluctant to present uncompensated ideas for fear that they will come across as inappropriate. So is it really worth taking the risk of crossing established boundaries? The answer is an emphatic "yes." When the customer sees that you have put in effort to offer a new perspective, they will know that you value the relationship—even if they're not thrilled with the idea itself.

Adding value

The idea you offer up doesn't have to be related to business and it doesn't need to be Earth-shattering; however, it must add value—don't present an idea just for the sake of doing so. Your customer doesn't know that you're about to offer an uncompensated idea, so before starting, get their permission. Let them know you have been thinking about their situation and that you have an idea for them. Ask if they think it's appropriate for you to present it. Most customers will be intrigued. Next, express what you think their need is, presen t the idea, and explain its specific benefits. Be humble when you offer the idea and give credit to others whenever you can; there's nothing to be gained by trying to make the customer think that you're smarter than they are.

TIME YOUR TIPS

Uncompensated ideas are best unveiled at the end of the meeting, not the beginning. They offer a great way to end any meeting on a high note.

CASE STUDY

Going the extra mile

A training company was seeking bids for a new video system. They spoke to three potential suppliers, each of whom made good recommendations. There was little to choose among the three on price, quality, capabilities, and service agreements. While they were in the decision-making process, the salesperson from one of the three suppliers emailed an article that appeared in *The Wall Street Journal* that day about one of the training company's clients. The email was accompanied by a short note: "I'm sure you saw this, but just in case…". Without other differentiators, the salesperson who took the extra step won the contract.

Asking for feedback

You have delivered your presentation. Your customers nodded enthusiastically throughout, so your recommendations must have been right on track. Or so you think. The only way to be sure and to move to the next stage of the selling process is to ask your client for feedback. It's time to hear from them.

GET YOUR TIMING RIGHT
You can ask for feedback at any time in your presentation. It's best to wait until you are finished so you don't get derailed, but if you suspect that the customer has a strong concern, ask for feedback earlier.

Facing the music

Even seasoned salespeople will hesitate before asking the customer to respond to their recommendations. A lot of time went into getting to this point and the fear of rejection can be paralyzing. No matter how many times you tell yourself that it's not you that's being rejected but your product or idea, it's hard not to take it personally. But don't make the mistake of delivering your recommendation and then saying… nothing, and just waiting to hear from the customer. If you don't ask, you don't learn. Even if the answer may not be what you were hoping for, ask the question and move on.

Welcoming objections

When you ask for feedback, the response you get is usually an objection; you should accept now that people almost always object even when they are convinced they want to buy. There are complex reasons for this, and techniques for resolving objections will be explored in the next chapter. But for now, you should welcome the objection. If you had not given an opportunity for the objection to surface, it would have still existed in the customer's mind, and you would never have closed the deal. With the objection out in the open, you have a chance to work with the customer to resolve it.

Asking open questions

You will get better feedback if you ask the right questions. It's hard to rebound from a blunt "No" so use open-ended questions to elicit responses from the customer that you can work with. Your questions should not be manipulative, but should be straightforward: slippery sales patter like "Sounds pretty good doesn't it?" may antagonize the customer, so frame questions in a way that maintains the high level of dialogue that got you to this point.

"What do you think about our recommendation?"

"I've been talking for a while; now I'd love to hear from you."

"I would appreciate some feedback."

"I'd love to hear your reaction."

"So, what are your thoughts?"

"How does that sound?"

"Any questions?"

Chapter 4

Resolving objections and closing the sale

Resolving objections is often the most challenging part of the sales process—it can be uncomfortable and unpredictable. But understanding the situation and practicing your responses will help you perform well when you encounter resistance.

Understanding objections

Up to this point in the needs-driven selling model, your role has been that of facilitator and adviser. Now, when you start to encounter objections from the client, the role can feel a lot more like selling. However, there's no reason to freeze and miss the opportunity.

Making buying decisions

Most people object to a selling proposal even though they are interested in buying. It's human nature. The lesson to learn is that not all objections are as bad as they first appear, and most can be resolved.

So why do buyers object when they're ready to buy? Most are simply looking for reassurance from the salesperson; they want to feel like they are making good, thoughtful, reasonable decisions, and they don't want to think that they are being hasty or foolish. They know that they will start questioning themselves soon after they make the purchase.

You may have heard some of the terms associated with this phenomenon, such as buyer's remorse and cognitive dissonance*. When you make a decision to buy, especially when spending a lot of money, you may experience a sense of disequilibrium. Part of you feels good about the purchase, but part isn't so sure. It's not a comfortable feeling. Professional buyers are also subject to these feelings, so to protect themselves and feel like they are doing the right thing, they object—even when they may be ready to buy.

*Cognitive dissonance— *a feeling of tension that arises when you keep two conflicting thoughts in mind simultaneously.*

Reacting to resistance

Most salespeople react in one of three ways when faced with objections—becoming defensive, aggressive, or simply giving up. None of these is constructive, and none is likely to help you close the deal. To keep from falling into one of these traps, do what you do best—problem solve with the customer.

The three common responses to resistance

BECOMING AGGRESSIVE
This suggests that you must convince the customer you're right—and by implication that they are wrong. This doesn't encourage discussion.

GETTING DEFENSIVE
This sends out the message that the process is more about you than the client.

BECOMING PASSIVE
Giving up is worst of all. For all you know there may be considerable interest.

GET EXPERT HELP
Use all your resources when you encounter difficult objections. Consult with your colleagues and invite experts to the presentation if you need support in specific areas.

Approaching conflict

Dealing with customers' objections is less daunting when you stick to a process derived from proven conflict-management techniques. This helps you focus on the objective, maintain your professionalism, and curbs your tendency to react too quickly.

Before introducing the objection-resolution model, there are two assumptions that you need to accept. Firstly, many, if not most, objections are unfulfilled needs. Needs are motivational in nature and when you don't meet them to the customer's satisfaction, they usually appear later as objections. Put another way, if you don't discover all the needs, you risk being blindsided later by an objection.

The second assumption—which may seem counterintuitive—is that most objections indicate interest at some level. Indifference and apathy are the reactions you want to see least in response to your recommendations. When the client complains about something, at least they care about the outcome. Taking the customer's objection as a good sign will encourage you to work to resolve it. It's a healthy way to approach conflict

You don't have to accept these assumptions at face value, but work with them and decide later whether or not you agree.

IN FOCUS...
JUSTIFYING DECISIONS

People's desire to resolve the cognitive dissonance that accompanies buying decisions is illuminated by an observation from the advertising industry. A person is more likely to read an ad for a major purchase—such as an automobile—after they have bought the product than before the purchase. Reading the ad reinforces the correctness of the decision made in the buyer's mind.

Introducing the process

When you encounter resistance, start by acknowledging what the customer has said without responding to it with offense or defense. Next, ask questions to learn the totality of the objection. Make sure that you have heard and understood the entire issue. Review your understanding with the customer of what is troubling them. Sometimes, you will simply paraphrase the objection to clarify it; at other times, you will have to reframe the objection and transform it into a need that you can address. Next, address the concern as effectively as you can in order to resolve it. If the customer accepts your response, determine if there are other concerns. If there are, repeat the process. If there are none, close the sale.

Resolving objections is a linear process, similar in many ways to the needs-driven selling model as a whole. As with any other linear process, you don't have to use every step to succeed, but having a well-defined process to which to refer will help you deal with what most people find to be the hardest component of the sales process.

TIP

STEER TOWARD A SOLUTION
Think of yourself as a facilitator when you resolve objections. It's your job to lead the way as you navigate towards resolution.

ASK YOURSELF... ABOUT YOUR BUYING BEHAVIOR

You can learn about your client's attitudes by reviewing how you react when you make a significant purchase.

• What reasons do I come up with to delay or prevent a buying decision?
• How much is my behavior shaped by the salesperson?
• Do I object because it helps me feel more confident about my purchase?
• Do I object because I want to test the salesperson?
• How do I react to an aggressive sell?

Collecting the data

The first two steps in the objection resolution process are acknowledging the client's objections and asking them to elaborate on their concerns. Posing the right questions helps you collect the critical data you need to understand and deal with the customer's objection.

TIP

TRANSFER YOUR SKILLS

Acknowledging is more than just a tool in the selling process—it is a life skill. Use it with your significant others, colleagues, children, even strangers. When you acknowledge how someone feels, good things usually follow.

Acknowledging objections

Your goal at this point is to encourage your customer to open up about their objections. To begin this process, you should acknowledge their concerns: this doesn't mean agreeing with their objections (which would suggest a lack of conviction on your part) or implying that you disagree (which would set the scene for confrontation). Instead, simply recognize their right to object, demonstrate empathy, and show that you are amenable to discussing the situation. They will see that you are willing, and hopefully able, to solve the problem.

A good technique for acknowledging objections is to reflect the customer's own language in your response. Aim to paraphrase their objection, without being patronizing. For example, if they bring up the objection that your product is far too expensive, you could reply "I recognize that expense is a big concern for you."

Below are some examples of the types of phrases you can use to acknowledge objections:
• "I can see why…"
• "I appreciate that investing in our system may seem daunting…"
• "That's a fair question…"
• "I think I understand why you might feel that way based on what you've heard so far…"
• "I appreciate your candor…"
• "I guess I wasn't as clear as I wanted to be…"

Questioning the client

The customer's stated objections are often just the tip of the iceberg. They may not be expressing all their concerns, or may be masking their true objections. To get to the bottom of their concerns, you need to start asking questions. Keep these questions crisp, open-ended, and void of content, so that you don't "lead the witness." For example, if a client voices a general objection, don't ask, "Is it the price?" This will succeed only in making them suspicious of price—you will have given them another reason not to buy! Instead, try something like: "Could you be more specific?" This will encourage the customer to elaborate without giving them new reasons to object. Similar question phrasings include:
- "Would you please elaborate?"
- "Can you say a little more about that?"
- "How come?"
- "I'm not sure I understand. Could you clarify?"

TIP

BE RESTRAINED
Don't go too far in expressing your desire to work with a prospect— it can work against you.

ASKING QUESTIONS

⬆ FAST TRACK	❗ OFF TRACK
Being objective	Appearing judgmental
Staying in control	Displaying emotion
Asking open-ended questions	Asking leading questions or patronizing the client
Being straightforward	Being perceived as manipulative
Using appreciative phrases	Being an interrogator

Being sensitive

When you deal with the client's objections, don't forget that you are in conflict resolution mode and sensitivity on your part is not only desirable but critical. The questioning process must not seem like an interrogation—it needs to be a comfortable experience for the customer so he or she will explain their concerns and continue the dialogue. Like so much of what impacts the sales process, it's how you do it that matters most.

Accepting objections

Of course, there are times when you should agree with what the customer is saying, but without closing off the conversation. For example, if your product is more expensive than the competition's and you are unable to shift on price, your reply could be: "Yes, it is expensive, but I hope you think it's worth discussing its cost in respect of what it can do for you."

Q IN FOCUS...
CROSSING THE LINE

Almost any positive behavior can become a negative one when used in excess. It's great to be curious until you become nosy. You should be assertive but not aggressive. By all means be pleasant; but stay away from obsequious. Be empathetic and customer focused, but don't appear patronizing. Take a position, but don't become dogmatic. And, of course, be tenacious, just don't get stubborn. These distinctions become particularly important when resolving conflict, but if you trust your instincts and build on them with experience, you'll be right a lot more than you'll be wrong.

BE POSITIVE
Let your customer know that you appreciate their insights by interspersing your questions with appreciative phrases such as: "Thank you" and "That's very helpful."

BE DIRECT
Clearly signal your intentions using phrases such as: "I'd like to ask another question or two in order to..." to make the climate more conducive to problem solving.

Encouraging the customer to open up

INTRODUCE YOUR QUESTIONS
Give reasons for why you need the information to help to diffuse suspicion and put the customer at ease. If your customer raises the objection that your solution is complicated, respond with: "Yes, it is complex—but it's also very manageable. Can we discuss this further...?"

MIRROR THE CLIENT
If the client becomes obstructive and puts you on the wrong foot, try mirroring his or her objections. For example, counter "Your suggestion is ridiculous" with "Why do you think this seems ridiculous?" Do this in a nonjudgmental way that conveys your real curiosity about the answer.

BE SILENT
Sometimes, and especially when a client reacts in an inappropriately strong manner, being silent is the best option. Silence can defuse the situation and give the client time to realize that his or her behavior is not contributing to a resolution.

Reframing objections

By this time, you have heard the customer's objections to your proposal. Most—but not all—objections that you will hear from clients are really disguised, unfulfilled needs. So the next step of the selling process is reframing* the objections as needs.

Translating into needs

*Reframing—*the art of turning a negative into a positive, changing the apparently unresolvable into the possible.*

Objections from customers are barriers to progress, whereas needs are aspirational, so it follows that turning objections into needs makes them easier to discuss and resolve. These examples illustrate how objections, in fact, mask needs:

• A client complains about the high complexity of your proposal: what he may need is a clearer explanation pitched at his own level.
• A client recounts a bad experience of a purchase similar to the one you are proposing: what she may need is reassurance that it won't happen again.
• A client laments the difficulty of changing their in-house systems: he may need to understand that you can help to facilitate the process.

SALESPERSON
Naturally, you need to know that the work is secure in our hands

SALESPERSON
There's a need to identify tasks that demand close collaboration

You can reframe almost any objection into an invitational question that asks how something can be done as opposed to why it can't. An objection like "My manager will never go for this" becomes "It appears to me that there's a need to establish a rock-solid business case for this purchase."

When you reframe a client's objection you are changing the tone of what they said, and you should avoid putting words into their mouth—note the use of "it appears to me" in the example above.

Setting objectives

When you reframe the concern as a need, make sure it is a need that you are able to address. For example, don't say something like "It seems like you need to get a lower price" if you can't move on price. Instead, try "As I understand it, you need to see more clearly the cost/value equation here."

After you have reframed the objection, confirm with the customer that they agree with your interpretation. You have now converted their objection into a new objective—with the client's agreement you can now move toward meeting the objective and edge closer to closing the deal.

CASE STUDY

Reframing for success

Reframing is not restricted to selling situations. A multibillion dollar company was in the process of selecting a new CEO: during the interviews, one of the leading candidates was challenged by the chairman. The candidate had a reputation for risk taking, and the chairman expressed his worries about his judgment in financial decisions. The candidate's reframe went something like this: "My impression is that you're concerned about my reputation for trying new things and need to feel comfortable that when it comes to financial decisions I will demonstrate the fiduciary responsibility that the job demands. Is that correct?" He gave a great response and two days later he got the job.

Discussing price

Customers will always complain about price. Indeed, price resistance is the most common objection salespeople will encounter and can be the hardest to resolve. However, as with other types of objection, understanding why the customer is objecting and turning that objection into a need can be an effective way of managing the resistance.

BE CLEAR ABOUT THE VALUE
Don't confuse price with value: people are always willing to pay more if they understand the value they are getting for their money.

Understanding price resistance

Everyone wants to find a good deal and feel like they are getting a good price. However, objections about price are sometimes used as a convenient reason to object, but are really a smokescreen to mask other issues. In these situations, it is important that you question your customer to determine what the underlying issue really is. At other times, however, the objection truly is all about price. In instances where the buyer is making his or her decision on price alone, there may be little leeway for negotiation, and you may choose to walk away from the relationship.

Preempting the objection

If you have undergone a thorough needs determination, when you make a recommendation your customer should not be surprised or shocked about the price. Needs determination should include a discussion of what the customer is currently paying or expects to pay. Questioning the customer about their budget or pricing guidelines will help you recommend a price that is close to what is expected. If the customer won't answer your questions, give them a "sense of" cost: "Just so you know, a program like this typically costs $100. How does that sound?" You will quickly find out whether this is a long way from what they expect to pay.

Resolving price objections

The objection-resolution process is your best tool in dealing with price objections. Firstly, acknowledge the objection as you would any other, for example: "I know you are trying to keep costs down." Next, get the customer talking. Ask questions, and find out about any other offers they have had from your competitors—how do they compare to yours? Are the deals comparable with yours in terms of the value delivered? Learn as much as you can regarding how far off you are in price from other offers.

When resolving price objections, reframing the objection is critical. Do everything you can to turn your customer's objection into a need, using phrases such as: "So if I understand you correctly, you need to know what you will get for the additional 10 per cent," "My understanding is that you need to know why we charge a bit more than Company X and why it's still in your interest to buy from us…," or "It appears to me that you need to feel comfortable with your decision to pay us more than some of our competitors…"

If the customer agrees with your reframe, go ahead and address the need. Give it your best shot, and see if they will accept your point of view. You will be surprised at how an objection often turns out to be less significant than it originally appeared to be.

TIP

CHOOSE YOUR QUESTIONS CAREFULLY

Getting a customer to elaborate about price or cost issues is a delicate matter. Be sensitive in your approach, using questions such as "How far off are we?" or "Can you tell us a bit more?"

IN FOCUS... LOWERING YOUR PRICE

The last thing you should do is lower your price without taking something off the table. If you provide a quote and a customer objects, and you then subsequently drop your price, the message is clear—you were charging too much originally. This sentiment can have serious negative impact on further business and your customer's perception of you. If you do have to lower the price (which happens), let the customer know what you have to remove or reduce from the original proposal. As a last resort, let them know you are lowering the price to earn your way in, but that the original price was fair and this is a short-term offer that you will not repeat.

Responding to objections

Once you have reformulated your customer's objection into a need, it's time to respond. Usually, this is straightforward—the answers lie in what you have already proposed and in knowledge you already have—but sometimes you will need to be creative to lead your client to a solution.

Playing to your strengths

Before you can move to the final stage of the selling process—closing—you need to deal definitively with the customer's objections (or unfulfilled needs, as we know them) by using all means at your disposal (see opposite). If you still cannot not resolve the objections, you need to revert to problem-solving mode. If you still draw a blank, call a time out and ask to come back in a day or two with fresh ideas to move forward. Your customer will respect you for it in the long run.

BE RELAXED

Remember that customers ask some questions that are not objections— simply plain questions. Just because someone asks you about inventory issues doesn't necessarily mean they are worried about them.

Mopping up the concerns

Your final act in the objection-resolution process is to learn if there are other objections. This may sound like opening Pandora's Box, but it's critical. If other objections do exist, you need to learn about them because if you fail to uncover them now, they will certainly spoil the deal later. So ask the question. Keep your inquiry neutral and use expressions like: "Is there anything else we need to discuss?"
Try to stay away from negative language and terms such as "objections" or "issues" or "concerns." If you use words like these, you can give the customer the impression that you know something that they don't. Keep it simple. If objections remain, go back and repeat the process until you have removed all the obstacles in the way of closing.

CREATE CONFIDENCE IN YOUR SOLUTIONS
Review similar problems that you have solved for other clients.

Closing in on closing

HIGHLIGHT THE SPECIFIC BENEFITS
Repeat or rephrase a benefit that the client has forgotten or did not fully appreciate during the earlier presentation phase.

REVIEW THE FEATURES AND BENEFITS
Go back over these trusted selling tools.

SELL YOURSELF
Make your customer feel confident in your ability. Explain why you're so well placed to address their concerns about service, quality, or specification.

SELL YOUR COLLEAGUES
Make sure that the customer knows that you're part of a dedicated and responsive team.

GET CREATIVE
Generate ideas together with your client to modify the strategy: use inclusive language when describing how to overcome objections: "we have to figure out why..." or "our priority is now to...."

SELL YOUR COMPANY
Talk about your company's history, successes, and commitment to excellence.

Closing the sale

Over the years, salespeople's ingenuity has given life to scores of "surefire" closing techniques. Going by names such as the Puppy-dog Close, the Distraction Close, and the Treat Close, some are just gimmicky, while others border on the manipulative. Their faults lie in the fact that they all see closing as a special technique, rather than the natural outcome of a problem-solving dialogue with the client.

BE GRACIOUS
Always thank the customer for their business—it is the classy thing to do.

Approaching the close

You have built the relationship, determined the needs, made great recommendations, and resolved the customer's objections. It's time to close—to ask for the business. So why do so many sales professionals find this step so difficult? The answer is simple—it is that fear of rejection rearing its ugly head once again. This fear pushes many experienced salespeople toward canned "closes," like the Specific Terms Close, where the idea is to present the customer with a prearranged buying scenario, and then ask them to agree to it. For example: "We can deliver 10 palettes on May 12 for $1,000—is that OK?" Of course, on occasion, this approach—and others in a similar vein—may bring about a sale, but often the customer will think you are being presumptive and rude. It's canned selling at its lowest.

Assuming the best

To close a deal you shouldn't need to rely on corny closing tactics. You need simply to demonstrate the same credibility, integrity, and degree of interaction with the customer that you showed throughout the selling process. Don't change the basis of your hard-won relationship at this point.

Assume that if the customer does not have a reason not to buy, he or she is ready to buy. This is called the Assumptive Close. In this Assumptive Close, the dialogue with the customer is very direct, and goes something like this:

SALESPERSON:
"Anything else we need to discuss?"

CUSTOMER:
"No, not that I can think of."

SALESPERSON:
"So everything seems OK?"

CUSTOMER:
"Yes, I believe so."

The point is clear even though the words you choose may vary: you ask the customer if there are other concerns. If they say no, you double check. If everything seems OK, just ask for the business.

SALESPERSON:
"Great, then how do we get started?"

Asking and getting

If you've done your job well up to this point, the customer will know that you have something valuable to offer and will want to buy from you; moreover they'll want you to ask for their business. If you don't, you're expecting the customer to do your job. It seems obvious, but if you don't ask for the business, you're much less likely to get it.

Planning for completion

Once there has been a commitment to buy, close the sale by beginning to pin down the specifics. A good way to cover all the key variables is to answer the "four Ws"—who will do what by when with help from whom? When you have the answers to these questions, you are ready to execute.

If you don't close the deal—and, of course, you won't always—it is vital to keep the momentum of the selling process going. Set objectives for resolving issues and be clear about what has to be done before the next meeting. Experienced salespeople will tell you that the only time you fail in a sales call is when you don't get a next step.

Consolidating the close

Everyone needs reassurance after making a large purchase—to silence the nagging voice asking if they did the right thing (discussed earlier in this chapter). With this in mind, it is important to make sure that you are highly visible to the customer after you have closed the deal. Some salespeople say that "the real selling starts after you get the business," and it's hard to argue with the sentiment. With hard work, anyone can get the first order; it's the ones who get the second, third, and fourth who are the most successful. Whatever you do, don't fall into the stereotypical image of a "love 'em and leave 'em" salesperson. If you do, your relationship will be a short one. Guaranteed!

To be successful repeatedly, you need to acknowledge the transfer of power that occurs when the deal is closed. When a customer is a prospect, they hold all the cards, but once they commit to the deal, they lose some of that power because they are dependent upon you to deliver. It's uncomfortable for them, and it is a good reason for you to show humility after closing the deal—it's not the time to whoop and punch the air.

Collecting for success

There is a distasteful acronym out there in the world of selling—ABC, Always Be Closing—that reflects the strong emphasis placed on closing by many sales managers. Of course, closing is important, but it shouldn't be viewed as an isolated goal. Transform this unhealthy acronym into an ABC that will help you—Always Be Collecting: only when you consistently question, understand, and resolve issues together with your customer will you be on the road to success.

TIP

JUST ASK

Ask for the business, even if it feels uncomfortable. Research has revealed that customers rank asking for their business as the sixth most important reason for doing the deal.

CASE STUDY

Using a "closer"

A young salesman had called on the same client twice a month for two years. Sensing he was close to his first order, he brought his boss with him. The junior salesman reviewed price agreements, credit terms, and product specifications with the client. He kept asking the customer if everything was approved, whether they were satisfied, and if there were any other questions. All the answers were positive, but the salesman just couldn't pull the trigger. Finally, the manager lost patience and blurted out

"Well then, how about an order?" The customer's response was "What took you so long to ask?"

The customer was obviously ready to buy and the young salesman's reluctance to close was only raising suspicions in the client's mind. If the manager hadn't stepped in, the sale could have been lost.

However, using a more senior person as a "closer" is a poor selling model: the salesperson should feel adequately equipped, trained, and empowered to ask for the business.

Moving beyond the close

After you have closed, you earn yet another great opportunity to differentiate yourself from the competition. Following through goes beyond just following up on your promises—doing what you said you would do professionally and on time. Following through means exceeding what's expected of you and so sending the clear message to your customers that you are consistently thinking about them.

Following up

Follow-up is doing whatever you committed to do at the end of the sales meeting with your customer. It is a process that you initiate to ensure that objectives are accomplished and commitments are fulfilled. It is your responsibility to make sure that all of your organization's resources are doing what is needed to move the relationship to the next level. Will the samples be there on time? Is everyone aware of and able to meet the agreed upon delivery dates? Is the team committed to participate in the next meeting?

Every single sales call you make—from a brief catch-up meeting to a formal presentation—deserves a follow-up letter. This can be a letter, an email, or even a handwritten note—whatever suits both your style and the occasion—but must follow every call.

 IN FOCUS... TRACKING CONTACT

Time speeds by. It's not hard for 90 days to pass before you realize that you haven't made any contact with a customer. "Out of sight… out of mind" may be a cliché, but it's true: and if you haven't been in touch with a client, it's a safe bet that your competitor has. To prevent long silences, track how often you make contact with your customers. Use a spreadsheet, graph paper, or whatever suits your style to record every face-to-face meeting, as well as phone calls, letters, and emails.

The letter should thank the customer for their time, review what was discussed, and define the next steps. It can also serve as a reminder of who committed to do what by when.

Following through

When you follow through, you do more than you need to. Here are some ways you can surprise your customers with your level of commitment:
• Regularly check how things are progressing internally, and communicate effectively to everybody involved on a day-to-day basis.
• Send your customers a list of follow-up activities and deliverables, including dates; make sure you meet them consistently.
• Let your customer know well in advance if for some reason you can't meet a deliverable.
• Send emails updating your customers without requesting a response. This instils confidence that you have their interests in mind all the time.

MAKING THE MARK

FAST TRACK	OFF TRACK
Promising and delivering	Overpromising and underdelivering
Putting it in writing	Assuming the customer understands
Being visible	Being a nuisance
Being consistently professional	Forgetting details
Showing interest in doing business	Appearing desperate or overanxious

Index

Acknowledgments

Dedication
I dedicate this to my family, who are by far the most important people in my life. Everything good that has happened to me begins with Lois, my wife of almost 40 years. She is my best friend, my consistent source of inspiration, my biggest cheerleader, and my stabilizing influence. She is also the nicest person I know.

My daughters, Andrea Cooper and Deborah Rubin, are living proof that your children do, in fact, grow up and become your best friends. Everything I do in life is magnified by the joy they provide every day. Their husbands, Jon and Howie, are marvelous citizens of the world and their spectacular children, Logan, Sage, and Jonah, generate feelings that I could not possibly put into words.

Author's acknowledgments
I begin by thanking cobalt id, who enabled me to put in writing much of what we have learned from our research during the last 30 years. Marek Walisiewicz has been an outstanding resource, and I am most grateful to him for his support.

I am gratified and thrilled that Dorling Kindersley chose to publish this book, as I have always admired this extraordinary organization.

Stephanie Katz is an outstanding editor who can transform the dullest verbiage into an interesting story. I admire her skills, appreciate her friendship, and thank her for her contributions.

Francine Mendence and Doris Anderson run The Baron Group and have stretched even beyond their extraordinary limits to help make this happen.

And finally, whenever I look at what I have been able to accomplish, all roads lead to Synectics® Inc. and the five wonderful years I spent at that marvelous organization. Rick Harriman, my dear friend and colleague, made that possible, and I will never stop expressing my gratitude to him.

Publisher's acknowledgments
The publisher would like to thank Hilary Bird for indexing, Judy Barratt for proofreading, and Charles Wills for coordinating Americanization.

Picture credits
The publisher would like to thank the following for their kind permission to reproduce their photographs:

1 iStockphoto.com: Steve Dibblee; 2–3 iStockphoto.com: Bubaone; 4–5 iStockphoto.com: John Boylan; 12–13 Alamy Images: Pokorny/f1 online; 14–15 iStockphoto.com: Suprijono Suharjoto; 22–23 iStockphoto.com: Julien Grondin; 26–27 iStockphoto.com: Eliza Snow; 29 iStockphoto.com: Jennifer Borton; 32–33 iStockphoto.com: Mark Evans; 35 iStockphoto.com: Terry Wilson; 37 Corbis: Klaus Hackenberg/zefa; 41 Corbis: Joel W. Rogers; 43 iStockphoto.com: Adam Derwis; 44 iStockphoto.com: Roberta Casaliggi; 49 Corbis: Guntmar Fritz/zefa; 51 iStockphoto.com: Paul Kline; 57 Science Photo Library: Michael Clutson; 58 iStockphoto.com: Mehmet Ali Cida; 63 Corbis: David Madison; 66 iStockphoto.com: Cyrop.

Every effort has been made to trace the copyright holders. The publisher apologizes for any unintentional omission and would be pleased, in such cases, to place an acknowledgment in future editions of this book.